BLACK

By

THE LOST POETS

PREFACE

"Rejoice and shout with laughter
Throw all your burdens down,
If God has been so gracious
As to make you black or brown
For you are a great nation
A people of great birth
For where would spring the flowers
If God took away the earth?
Rejoice and shout with laughter
Throw all your burdens down
Yours is a glorious heritage
If you are black or brown "
(Rejoice, Gladys Casely Hayford 1904-1950)

Gladys Casely-Hayford's poem, in its simplicity is the epitome of this whole anthology. The perpetual need and hunger for rejoicing and all forms of self-love in the color of our skins as blacks, regardless of our nationality or geographical locations, is one that has long been subdued until recent times. Expressionism was once seen as outcast or illegal for black folk and as such the imagery of the beauty of blackness in all its entirety - language, love, poetry, prose and all its passion – was a figment of the imagination. This anthology, combining the works of young black poets from different walks of life, religions, nationalities, personal beliefs and fears serves as a confluence of sorts rooted in the simple undeniable fact that an awakening is needed for those seeking to have their voices heard.

The Lost Poets initiative was born out of the need for expression in all its forms, the need to embrace diversity and the strengths we tend to possess when we do both. All collections by this initiative combined works of young poets that are in the now, not dwelling in pasts but in the real present. We intend to amplify voices into a single voice speaking against conforming to pasts long buried but collectively joining heads and hands in bettering ourselves and birthing a new culture; One where our voices matter too.

The materials which form the inspiration for this anthology can visibly be seen as modern in that they are different amongst themselves. To start with, there is a departure from the obsessive public themes of black violence or independence. Here, the poets dwell on their common yet different searches for identity. This quest, as you may call it, is an almost inescapable one owing to the fact that black poetry was always based on the need to fight and be free. But, now this book takes us into the supposed nirvana of freedom, unraveling turmoil, tempests and temptations at every turn. It uncovers in a single collection the travails of a black man or woman in our present age and time.

This anthology is a testament calling readers to take a piece of its body, wielding truths and tales never told, rhythms seldom heard and the unflinching gospel of what it takes to be black.

Osalam C. Wosu
Afrikana Web, 2019

LIST OF CONTENTS

DEVELOPMENT OF POWER
    Balance
    Black grapes
    Nous sommes noirs
    The cycle
    What she made
    Sunday mornig mantra
    Don't settle
    Little prince
    Spirituality
    Jails
    Home within
    You're beautiful
    Hey
    Arewa Arewa

ORGANIZING WINS
    What greed is worth

MEANINGFUL IMPACT
    Scavenger
    Oddly enough
    Antidote
    The hate we give
    Last summer
    Broken plates

Dear sun
Melanin
I write to tell you
Streetlights
Say freedom
How to enslave

PARTICIPATION AND MEMBERSHIP
Fit outs
The truth in the stars
Who's king?
Forgive me for keeping you waiting
Empire state of mind
BLACK

ONGOING REFLECTION AND INNOVATION
Freedom and slavery
Wreck
Questions
Embrace
Off-centered
Expose
A black woman's soul gone rouge
This world has made me so
If love is human
Car race
Hide
No changes
Lost

ABOUT THE POETS
    Osalam C. Wosu
    Adegunloye Kayode
    Salim
    Priye (K. O)
    Vincent (Vincethapoet)

DEVELOPMENT OF POWER

Balance

Astronomical science explained the impossibility of days without nights
Chinese famous symbol of yin and yang depicts in perfection the serene blend of black and white
Who will see the existence of humanity without my black self?
Who will say there can be a meaning of white without black to balance it?
Me, us, them, are all essential
Balancing the universe by my color is a purpose
I am beautifully embracing this purpose
This is the truth and I will believe nothing else.

Salim

Black Grapes

Upon a day in a field of greens and fruits and ornamental floras
my friend told me many times he had wished he was white
many times had wished his hair was golden with highlights
many times had wished he was born into another region of earth
many times had called himself ugly
but then he told me he was just little then
and he laughed at himself and raised his head to the sun
locked his eyes and said, "Such naivety."
Then he put down his head and opened his eyes.
His final words that minute before we left the field was,
"These black grapes never feel ashamed to grow
amidst red apples and white lilies
and see, Salim, they are indeed beautiful.
My God, we are very beautiful."

Salim

Nous sommes noirs

Blacks folks, no tokes
No speed like Bolt
We walk on the loke
Black blokes everywhere
Getting our renaissance
So we holla at our other brothers
And our sisters play poke
As for the other ones,
We don't care whether they bloat
Our goals are simply wassup!

Kayode Adegunloye

The cycle

"You ain't a warrior until you've killed a warrior," I once heard somewhere.
I Thought, 'Damn look at the loss. Is that why niggas pops' dead?'
In these families it's niggas gone or winners of brutal casualties
The hunter with blood thirst is haunted by mental faculties
Alone he sat a throne in jail
Thinking the future for the victorious victor is hell
All alone with no guidance his son goes on to rebel
He's only known as the son of a warrior who failed
Now he's feeling distress and all he knows is he's the son of a nigga who's real
So he like, "Fuck all this fighting. I'm about to show these niggas who's real.
Done lived my whole life as a hybrid [a Christian willing to kill]
Better close your eyes you don't wanna witness or watch shit get wicked for real."

Vincethapoet

What She Made

Moms listen, I know we kept it different
like I was a man cause you ain't want me to be imprisoned
 instilled a message in me that said 'love first'
My moms worked enough to show love hurts
That OG who had a plan to save 5 kids, cause she ain't wanna
see them doing like the streets did or worse,
I saw the truth at an early age
almost drove em wild with rage- clip the disconnect short circuit
the main
he can't be tame when he spazzing out
this hip hop but you can tell that the Jazz is loud
I crash the house and take the city captive
the pastor bout' singing praises of a lowly route
then be showin out in the pastures with the holy cows,
he floatin now: bro ' gone tell'em the flow about.
holding those close who know that holy thou is only in the soul
of those giving more than holding out less roll it out, "if you
ain't talking cash what you talking bout?"
I'm calling out the kats who got the youngest mouth

Vincethapoet

Sunday Morning Mantra

Manifest! Manifest! Manifest!
Let her peace be bliss.
Make her joy abundant.
Give her wisdom to pick kings out of young men.
Make her roots grow till time indefinite.
Stretching as far and deep as the galaxies between.
I am queen.
I am queen.
I AM Queen!
Mother Earth time maker. Goddess embodiment.
Make known the way.
Lead from within.
You are not defective!
You will win!

Vincethapoet

Don't Settle

Why black peoples always gotta settle?
I say hell No!
They jail folks
And say be broke less you ready to sell soul!
I say hell No!
I sell gold.
And give a stare that's pale cold.
I say hell No!
They jail folks
And say be broke less you ready to sell soul!
I say hell No!
I sell gold.
And give a stare that's pale cold.
I say hell No!
They jail folks
And say be broke less you ready to sell soul!
I say hell No!
I sell gold.
And give a stare that's pale cold.

Vincethapoet

Little Prince

Before
 the age of adolescence
and nature robbed me of my childhood
my little innocent imagination never fathomed
 the distance between poles, nor the variation of race on earth.
I knew
only Minna my darling birth town
the Middle East Arabian channels that was aired
 on the bulged TV screen then, the ignorance that enveloped
my innocence
believed they were mere TV fictions
like the collections of my animated Disney CDs
 in mum's room
I am sure we all were that kid that knew
 no such thing like variation of race too. At our one year or two
or three years
of being mortals enslaved to air
the Nigerian anthem I learnt from my Nursery school
 that I still sing like it is the anthem of humanity/ so oft rang
with immense nostalgic energy.
 It says *"unity"* at the end of it
I know that word well since four years old
Now
 I know words
like "xenophobia"
and "racism"
Now
 I know

compound words like "African America"
and "Afro-Latin Americans"
being black
 is the sin our fellow humans out there never made
coming from a race they never signed for is now their crime?
These questions
 I asked
 my inner world many times
but
 I wonder
if the outside world will ever answer fairly.

Salim

Spirituality

From the days of my spiritual slumber
I was housing the dream of becoming a notable scientist
to play with theories of numbers and codes
Then I fell in love with astronomy, theories of universe and space walking
this became a dream and I began to find my geography classes interesting
but my soul's fountain of knowledge grew a deeper learning in it
is it the theories of the universe or planet universe
is it the theories of planet earth or country earth
My soul's deepness found a purpose from those dreams
to teach the kids in my society pro bono
to grow them up with deep sense of humanity and a bit of my soul's geographical idea
by morning light and noontide I shall tell them that
earth is our temporal home
all these continents we see are scattered limbs of earth
our close and distant relatives spread all over earth
I shall give them a poem to remember at night by moon or stars
or empty dark sky's vastness the poem will be with the lines succeeding this line
Do not call that continent "America" call it
"My American family"
Do not call that continent "Africa" Say "My African family"
Don't call them black, call them humans
Don't call them white, call them humans.

Salim

Jails

Colors that I know of at childhood were for fine arts mosaic,
leaf duplication and shading with reference to the sun's rage
but growing up and living in a world like this made me realize an illness
they are used for labeling humans by fellow humans
I saw the art of Mona Lisa painted with many colors
all blending in serene unity
Leonardo Da Vinci knew this unity amongst many colors is possible
Colors blinding us from the truth that the red in all of us is unity enough
Was it my own crime to unconsciously pick a skin color at the freedom of inexistence?
But the world out there that do not wear same skin as mine
chose to sue me in the court of discrimination sitting in their minds
some even jailed me in a corner of their heart
The cell is with no number as a label
but with the word "BLACK" written on it in bold.

Salim

21

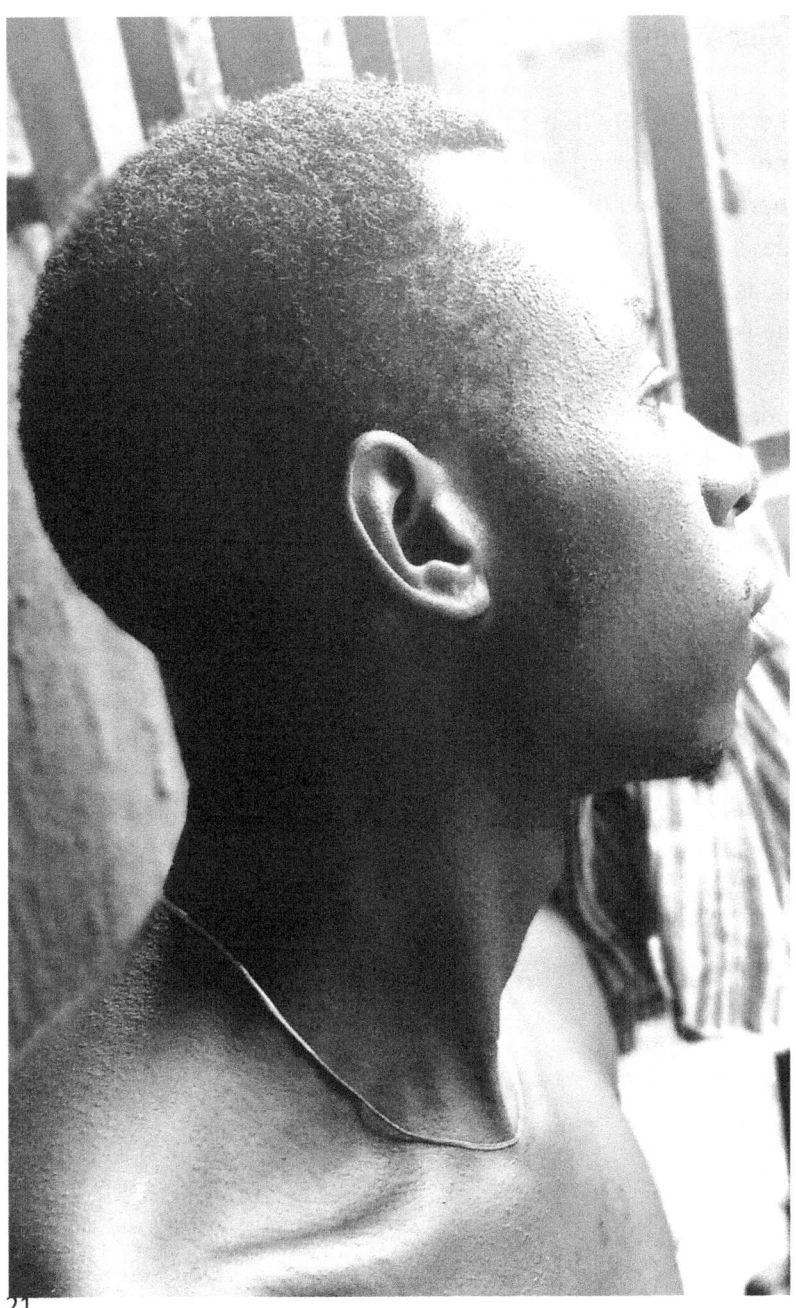

Home Within

There is a lovely home in loving yourself
find that home and breathe there my friend.
There are good things about finding that home
one is the freedom
one is the enjoyment of acceptance
one is the passion of mining deep to explore the treasure home
another is walking feeling like a treasure.
I accept myself and love myself
I am black and I love it and I enjoy all these good things within me
I am a beating mosaic made of graphite and black diamonds.

Salim

You're Beautiful

At first I thought to blame mama
Why she had to go down with a black man
When she knew she was black too
But as the time went by
I matured gradually
And as I grace the process, I saw reasons
I understood the beauty I carry
And I never felt like washing it away

Kayode Adegunloye

Hey

Hey black boys!
Hey black girls!
Yes! It's you I'm calling
Don't mince it one bit
Your melanin is beautiful
And it is respected intoto

Kayode Adegunloye

Arewa Arewa

The beautiful one
Open up for your love lagbaja
Lets have some fun
Arewa Arewa
I've come for your hand
Books won't take you far
I own 50% of this land
Arewa Arewa
Girls are not good in math
You cannot be an engineer
Boys own this class
Arewa Arewa
Architecture? Really?
What an awful construction of a car
And now you're into photography
Arewa Arewa
How many times do I call you?
Find a rich man
He'll solve all your problems for you
Arewa Arewa
She wanted to rule the world
But your words stung like a scar
She unconsciously made you all her lord
Arewa Arewa
You can be the greatest
They'll want to kill your star
But don't let them have it
Because Arewa you deserve it.

ORGANIZING WINS

What Greed is Worth

I'm cold like stiff particles.
Try to wet jack, I frost ya whole nautical.
Been not optional, leave or be left popsicle.
Mind drop diamonds, you crop to trying cop nickels.
Y'all think his thoughts fickle?
All about the act?
Not a pitcher with a mitt, just a nigga with a bat?
Might resort to back slapping, ask em "how they handle that?
I'm reporting from the street, no camera man in back.
If paper dreams was the need it'd be macks and G's fast asleep picturing fed greed.
Yo I know he think he god but his head bleed.
So what you saying? Why you playin?
Go head and kick it down.
Weapon is doubt!
Go without and have the most instead of showing out.
Dudes be clowns,
And don't know nothing bout the earth.
 She's a bitch who got kids, talk about some good dirt.
Niggas want out of the hood,
Remember she was hood first.
Before thirst, shorty was abroad, no skirt.
Some men got jealous, some put her ass to work.
Its people going through some shit, I say farming couldn't hurt.
Learn to grow the things you need, come to know what greed is worth.

Vincethapoet

MEANINGFUL IMPACT

Scavenger

Pain follows my heart as I search for my father's gravestone
Beneath this sea of dead leaves that paint peace in this place where
Tears have watered the ground to an orchard of regrets, words unsaid and toxic memories.

When a loved one dies, we seek life in places that offer silence as bread
And darkness like wine
We walk into the night away from queries and accusing eyes
Away from hands tapping shoulders and the sounds of empty embraces
Away from the silence of mourning
into the weeping, wailing rhythms that make up grief.

My mother will plant her hands in the pillows and sacrifice tears to conjure memories
My sisters will cry and look for my shoulder, to lean on,
even when I am a tree with roots hewn into a sad poem.
I will stand for them, by them,
Offer them peace, hope and all things they don't understand
And when I retire to my bed,
Pain will follow my feet as I search for peace too
Behind this sea of tears.

Osalam Wosu

Oddly enough

She was the odd one amongst everyone
Illuminating the class
But no one ever cared
I sensed the awkward feeling she manages
But while she wished to be like us
I quietly went close to her tiny creamy white ears
And whispered
"We've been through this before
But we thrived,
So you can too…"
So thrive!

Kayode Adegunloye

The Hate We Give (THWG)

They say it's not the hate you give
But the hate we give,
How we loathe everything about this blackness
And how Khalil gets a bullet to the chest,
For reaching to get his hairbrush
Perhaps it would have been "hands up,"
If the suspect was white
But because our friend was black
He was left for dead
Only because he reached for a "weapon"
His hair brush!

Kayode Adegunloye

Broken Plates

The sound of the broken plates played in my head
What am I going to do? Oh golly! I'm dead
"John!" She called
"What was that?" She asked
"My left ear," I was tempted to say
Please don't come this way
Momma will spank me in ways I didn't deem possible
I had broken the plates that were irreplaceable
I heard her footsteps echo down the stairs
See you in heaven then, wish me well
Because my brain had forgotten how to work
What's that sound? Is it my heartbeat or it's a clock
Best thing is to kneel down on this broken pieces
That's the only way she would lighten this beating
"You broke my plate?"
The subtlety in her voice made me feel a little faint
"Clean it up," she muttered and walked away
Well, I guess this was my lucky day.

K.O

Dear Sun,

Sun please get out of my face
I am now darker before I get to my work place
My skin already has tar from above
Kindly reduce your wavelength by a single node
The other day someone said
I look like under the bed
I watch those other girls who for fair skin take meds
But I'm here begging so stop being a hot head
I don't blame you,
That would just be rude
And I'm not a fool
But please stop making me look like burnt wood
I want to thank you for understanding
Don't get me wrong, I appreciate all you've done
next time that on the pavement, I'll be standing
I will sing praises to you the sun.

K.O.

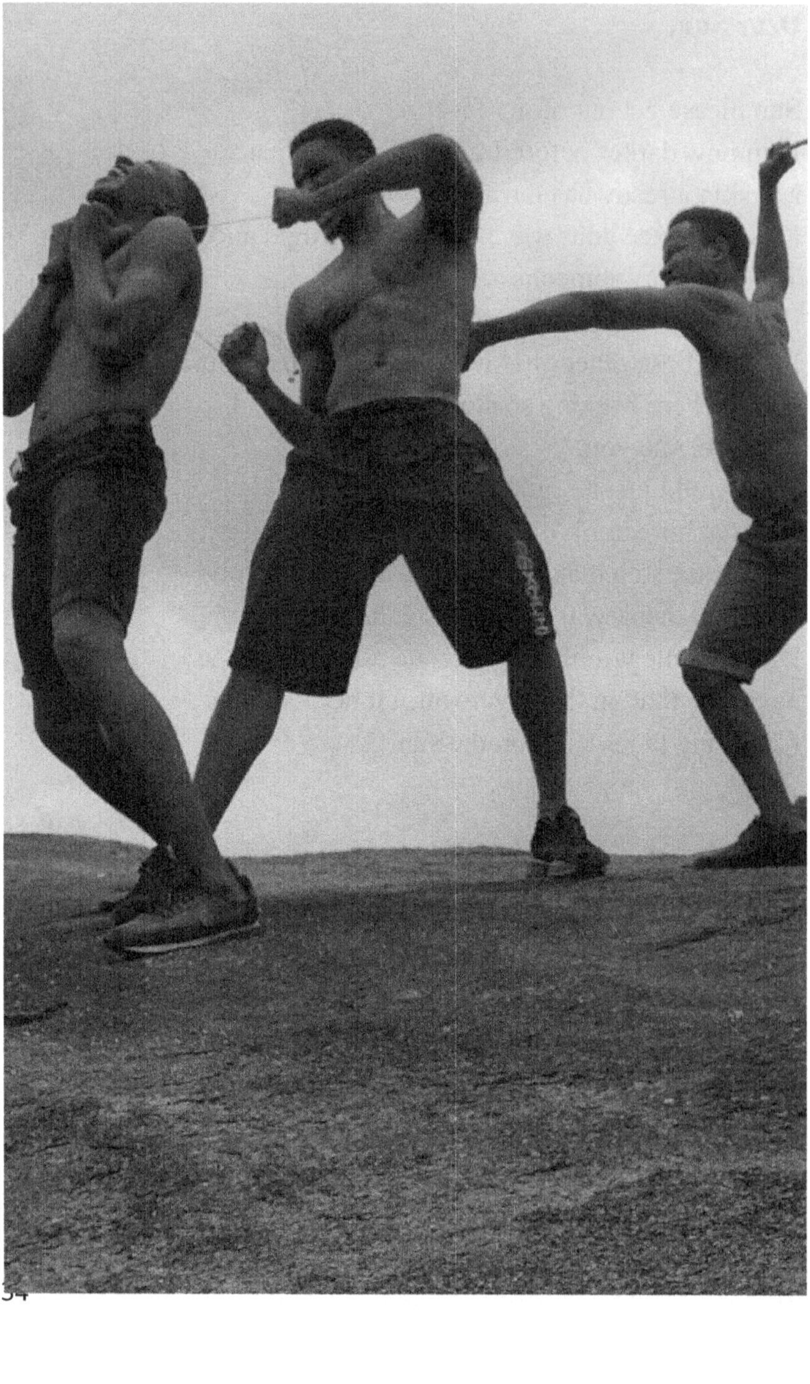

Melanin

A needle drove into my skin
A needle drove into your skin as well
Is it red blood I bleed?
The same you bleed as well?

A smile etched on my lips
One etched on yours to
I have white teeth or so it seems
And you have them too!

I Breath in. Breath out.
You breathe in and breathe out
Well, well, I'm definitely gonna say my thoughts out loud
It appears we both breathe oxygen in our nose and out our mouth

So tell me?
Is it melanin
That's in me
That makes you better…oh indeed

In case you don't know
You have a deficiency.

K.O

I Write To Tell You

I write to tell you that my bones are made of contention
And my skin black with discord
I write to tell you that I come from the dust
And I am situated between desires that threaten to break or mould me
I write to tell you how I yearn to learn the ways of water
And the strength of this earth
I write to tell you of my roots that were shattered
And how my fruits fled in fear.
I write to tell you I am searching for my father's face
Amongst this sea of bodies
I write to tell you I have swallowed poisons
Just to familiarize with pain
I write to tell you I have let light fall through my fingers like wheat
Just because I live freer at nights where sin is a norm.
I write to tell you this;
That though I am not the architect of the future
Or the steward of the past
I will stumble into the present searching for home
Even if I land in the arms of women that promise
To show me the world beneath the blanket of starless nights.

Osalam Wosu

Streetlights

Maybe in the middle of the night when the streets are drunk sleeping in gutters
I will try to hear the moans of the dead
And try to listen, if they found peace in their rest
After the shots were fired and their dead tongues lowered.
I will try to see in the night, the hope our leaders preached by day
And know if our future is tense
Because our present is not perfect and the past is what it is – lost.
Maybe in the middle of the night when these streets are made of loss
I will try to understand the stories of mothers
That watched their sons die under the streetlights
gun-in-hand, blood in mouth and snow on streets.
I will try to smell the spring scent that envelopes the city
In between sirens and the soul of alcohol
Drifting, sifting across the block
At day, at night.
Maybe in the middle of the night I will try and I will succeed
-to write a poem without tears away from this street of pain
-to listen to a song of smiles devoid of death
-to live without fearing the dark, waiting for hope
Waiting…
Under the dull streetlights.

Osalam Wosu

Say Freedom

On my tongues lives cities
Where boys and men go to die
Say Kano, say Lagos
And watch freedom burn in the street, maimed
Then you can understand why I lie mute
Why I have hidden my name beneath bushels
And my voice beneath my skin
Say Port Harcourt
And you will hear that 'outspoken' means dead.
I do not want to die
But in a land of night, light is sin
And no matter how long you hide
They will come by land, they will come cash in hand
Just to drown your voice and swallow your name.
When they do, say FREEDOM
And watch it burst forth from your mouth and break
The darkness into a land of rainbows;
And that is how to be black and free.

Osalam Wosu

How to enslave

He lay there
Lying bare
Like a slain bear
A king banished to a cave, where?
A land without his name.
"There, now surely he'll go insane."
Sever his braids to reduce his strength.
Then introduce him to insolent taste and wash his memories away.
Take precautions to change his ways
Without these feats he's far too great
Title him as a slave, as cattle, with equivocal worth of a kid.
Don't let him read!!!
This point is supreme
He must never know of the mountain of Tariq
Make Timbuktu a word of refuses,
Make Songhay a word of make-belief
He'll be so removed from Solomon's wisdom that it's possible he may start to believe.
Lie and lie then write those lies and sell those lies to those who'll lie some more.
If he can't see that he is king it's possible he'll never take up the sword.
The truth about trees is they watch over their seeds and give root whenever they leave.

Vincethapoet

PARTICIPATION AND MEMBERSHIP

Fit Outs

Fitting in has always been hard for them
They thought being a fit out is a flaw they should overcome
This is the infection growing up in a plaguing society
with discrimination of skin and race and ideologies of
labels put into them
Hearts and eyes blinded by colors
Like the worries of OJ Simpson to white Sue
Like nobles of the trying to avoid the birth of August 23rd
So many wrongs in our world
They are forced to feel like fit outs
I wonder if nature, true nature of a man should be his crime.

Salim

The Truth in the Stars

I looked at you through these two tired windows called eyes
I saw a structure of art – simply the kind of being that I am
I saw no mediocre labels like tribe or colors written in the handwriting on your forehead
I saw a brother, I saw a sister, a mother, a father
You are what my common self is
You are human and that is enough for me my friend
But will you look at me that way too?
Will you forget the color nature dyed my skin with?
Will you forget the faction nature placed me in?
Will you choose to look at me with your inner eyes?
They are the only pairs that see the truth
Will you choose to carry me in the heart of your heart?
It is the only masterpiece that knows the truth
What is that truth you ask
Write your question on a golden color paper and tie it to an arrow
Shoot it into the vast blue with sun or dark with halo
You shall see it explode like New Year's fireworks revealing to you the golden truth
"Humanity needs love from all her humans, by all her humans and to all her humans"
Banish discrimination will you my friend?

Salim

Forgive Me for Keeping You Waiting

The sun and his moon luminate their space.
Harmonizing one another, fortifying each other's faith.
Nights grew dark as days grew great.
Battles were lost, Kings were called slaves.
Still the strength of their love was sweet to the taste.
Evil and hate couldn't conquer the pair.
"But would the sun still glow if the moon wasn't there?"
"And the moon being rock was tough under pressure,
but without her sun could she keep the stars together?"
Evil and Hate conspired a plan.
"Call the moon woman. Call the sun a man."
Hate was infuriated that Evil had lost battles so she said, "Call
the moon a wench, and call the sun cattle."
So They yelled it and yelled it. till the people got wind.
Then the people saw the sun and seen him as man. What's worse
is they listen to evil's beckoning voice.
So whom they use to call king, they now know as "boy."
The moon got it worse, because Hate hated her soul.
So she taught the moon's stars that the moon's beauty was old.
She fashioned the stars in her Indian wigs.
Until it was hard to tell if the moon and stars were kin.
But Hate didn't stop, she wanted the sun for herself.
Because the sun knew love and Evil loved wealth.
As time passed slowly and the moon grew alone,
the once luminated rock had turned to cold stone.
She wondered what happened to the sun? Where did he go?
Had he forgotten about our time in space?
Had he become over whelmed by a space in time?

She longed for her stars, she feigned for his shine.
Someday became one day and that day went by.
The sun had returned brilliantly bright from the things he had learned.
Seeing his moon in her altered state.
He vowed to give her glow no matter how long it would take.
He told her to stand up and repeat after him, "My glow is love, my love is breeze just like the wind in the trees my glow is unending."

Vincethapoet

Empire State of mind

Empire State of mind
Revenue is devil use our asset is time
Rebel! Rebel! Rebel! You might as well Rebel!
Stop wasting time
Go save a mind
Unshade the blind
A stratification system is the system's existence denied
Collectively defy to conquer and divide
We need a perspective team
Tell any seed you see to focus on the green, that Mother Nature gave to us as men.
Also let him breathe and educate him if he doesn't read
The new agenda is to supersede the eye that super sees to it our every move is tailored to the T.
Know what you think and prepare yourself for the war to break out on a brink.

Vincethapoet

BLACK

They say, black don't crack
But there will come a time
When black will crack
And beneath it won't be slugs and slime
Because black is black
So it'll be like the luxury of old wine
Because beauty is black
Please ignore the rhyme
And listen to the truth and fact
Black is bold and ever so fine
Black is a deeper dark
Black is like
The lessons we lack
Black is you, black is I.

K.O

ONGOING REFLECTION AND INNOVATION

Freedom and Slavery

It is said that we are prisoners of our nature
but she is a free creature to her nature.
When she smells slavery in anything
her next breath will be with the thought of breaking out.
So her skin is as dark as dark
her natural skin is black.
She never thought of breaking out.
To kill her beautiful melanin and drown herself in rejection
That is not breaking out but slavery in tyranny!
Accepting her nature became her freedom
black was from the genesis of her thoughts
nothing but a queen like beauty.

Salim

Wreck

I never knew
           that the sea was the epithet of your love
That
     your words meander truths like rocks and
snatch my balance
That
     by day you welcome me with warmth and waves
 and drown me by night
That
when you fall you
     drag me down with you
     into
      a
     watery grave…

I never knew
           that the sea was the epithet of your love
And that
 the breeze you sent to capture me was poison
And you embraced me, just so you could know how
Deep I could dive before coming up for air

I never knew, my Nubian lover
And now even though I drown,
My heart still finds a way to burn.

Osalam Wosu

Questions

When they asked me of Africa and home
I told them of cities that don't sleep,
with food and smiles hugging the night till dawn calls
Of the tiny fragments of love that envelopes us at the dinner table
with our hands plunged into a single bowl
Of the wet mornings in the farm and how we ran after bush rodents for a reason to brag to friends
Of how grandma sings when we unveil the new wrapper we bought
that glitters by day and jingles when she walks.

They ask me of Africa and home, and I lie, or rather I hide the real truth
The truth about war and mysterious affections
About love, lust and the uncountable strands of guilt that binds us
How we shiver at nights because of witches before we remember robbers exist
How religion is supreme and education is just a pastime
How deities eat by dawn when men sleep at the junctions
leaving empty pots of offerings when we walk to the filthy village stream.

When they ask of Africa, I don't lie, no
I just dream of blue skies and
All the opposites I wish we could be.

Osalam Wosu

Embrace

This is about embracing/
This is about finding freedom in the art you are
Dear soul this is about accepting and wearing your melanin casing called body.
"Black is beautiful, black is beautiful" I have heard us say this sentence so oft by sun and night
and on our captions too,
 but by our seaports, many cargos that fought and won sea tides are blissfully sitting
 there carrying many varieties of chemicals in their stomachs.
"Black is beautiful" we say so oft, but we import every idea and liquid
that will gently suffocate our dear melanin, we crave for a color change, I pity.
"Black is beautiful" we said, it is beautiful, forever and ever beautiful,
but only when we truly began to accept it in that apple in our rib cages
and deeply beyond shall we then see it as art.
Your black is beautiful, marry it.

Salim

Off-centered

My son said "heroes never win at last anymore"
And I know that sorrow has altered the denouement
"Little one, today is simileous to days of old
But personification and greed has breathed life into gold"
My poetry walks by on broken limbs
Satirical mirrors stand before me
And all I do is behold all others' sins.

    I speak with tears at every punctuation
    My diction is laden with words of injustice
    Happy endings have bequeathed our lives to Thespis
    Elisions omit not vowels but our flaws
    And free verse is restrained now, ravaged by tyranny's claws.

        Irony is cynosure, but to the grave it leads
        Hyperbole is sweet, but only our pride it feeds
        Tragedy kicks our groins at the nadir of the situation
        So, off-centered I write, my only consolation.

Osalam Wosu

Expose'

I want to tell no lies
That when she left,
a hole didn't materialize in my chest
That I was born black,
with heart so dark, love was lost in its halls
That I don't gorge on food like heartbroken women,
in the comfort of lonely rooms,
draining tear after tear.
I want to tell no lies
That slow songs don't reach
into my soul at nights and cradle my heart
till I feel like pain itself.
I want to tell no lies.

Osalam Wosu

A Black Woman's Soul Gone Rogue

Ain't no gain from a black woman's soul gone rogue. I heard it's what makes the snow cold. She was looking for love bold and made moves like the lava flow.
She heard stories about lots of hope and choose not to let her demons show.
Thinking most the time the things I know conflict with how I feel so I think I'll smoke and drink until I finally feel woke.
She toked the teal dope, sipped a coal and start spitting fire quotes like, "I'm thicker than lightning bolts" and "I'm really into frightening folks." She lost hold of life's handle and found herself in pride's scandal. Gradually becoming more jaded until she hated life's gentle.
So the tale is simple. Keep life at the right tempo and it'll be gold. Because there ain't no gain from a black woman's soul gone rogue.

Vincethapoet

This World Has Made Me So

Mother before you hallow my skin
With kisses and warm tears, tell me if I am a disease
This world has made me so.
Tell me why the evening swallows the sun with malice
This earth has taught me not to smile into light
For it might be fire that writes poems into skins
Of loved ones and sings it to the world in ballads.
Mother, before you wipe my skin
With your hands that drip with sweat
And smell of sweat and bruises
Tell me why my skin is dark
Like those mournful starless nights
When the chirps and chimes of nocturnals are swallowed whole
by the serpent moon.
Mother, before you go to rest
Tell me why my skin is coloured
Tell me why I am diseased
Tell me a prophesy of the future
Tell me if I am worthy of love
 I think no. Why?
Because this world has made me so.

Osalam Wosu

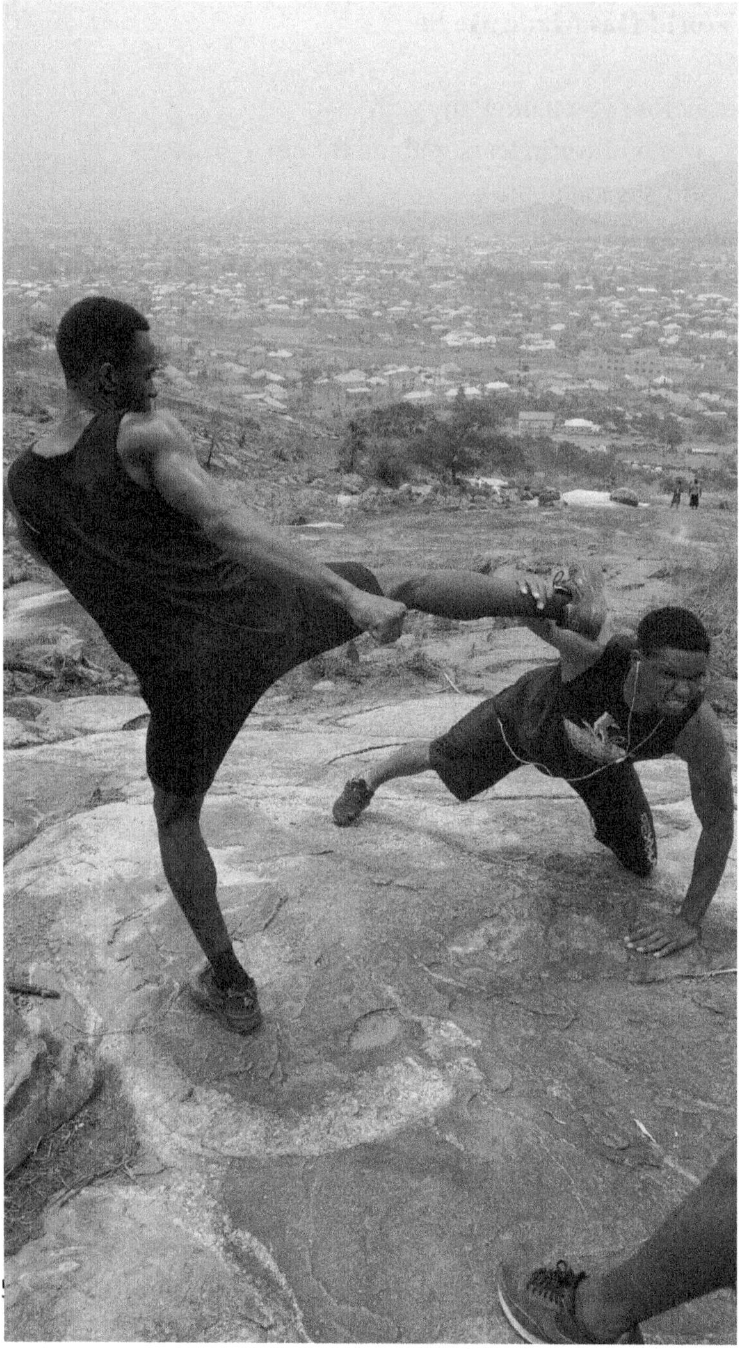

If Love is Human

If love is human – she will be a visible work of Art
Her skin color will be a serene blend of all that is present on earth
Her race will be humanity
Her tribe will be humanity too
And her religion must be love alone
 She will be a being born from all of us
For only then can she universally come to life
She will be born to all of us
For only then can she be a citizen of all nations
She will know no color madness but she will see it as an essential part of life
She will do no act of prejudice or racism
This love, isn't she what we all crave for?
Now won't we oblige to her beautiful path.

Salim

Car Race

The little white boy
Pushed his toy car down the rail
The little black boy
Pushed his toy car down the rail
The little white boy
Watched his toy car fail
The little black boy
Danced, not waiting for the audience to hail
The little white boy
Cried like a wale
The little black boy
Wondered why his opponent suddenly looked ill
The little white boy
Would not accept this fail
The little black boy
With his trophy had already begun to set sail
The little white boy
Said, "He is a cheating snail."
The little black boy
Was forced to return come rain, come hail
The little white boy
Pushed his toy car down the rail
The little white boy
Pushed the black boy's car in a pail
The little white boy
Did not fail
The little black boy
With tears in his eyes watched the audience hail.

Hide

I'm lost in all the hopes I had
My dreams were more than just plain and clad
My future held glories I hoped to behold
Stories die in my throat untold
I wanted so much more
Vowed my life would not be a bore
Vowed I would not be held by the same shambles
That only allowed my forefathers aspirations crumble
I dreamt so far and wide
I startled my own mind
Promised I won't be restricted to this hide
we call skin. But it's just social ladders they climb
Promised myself I would fight
Even with bleeding eyes I would fight and fight
Till I get to my apprehended height.

K.O.

No changes

The sky is so blue
The sun is so warm up high
And skin so dark

I really like this
It's gorgeous without stains to it
With skin so dark

They suddenly go pink
Even Yellow, green, red, white, orange
Just because they're sick

But I remain black
And despite all the troubles here,
I remain my black

Kayode Adegunloye

Lost

Like the night before this one, the heat was peaking
I found myself a bar and resorted to drinking
My head floated with thoughts while my life was sinking
That I didn't notice when the beauty across the bar started winking
For the pleasures of the night I had come, was what she was thinking
But she couldn't understand or see the pain in my cold eyes, lost and unblinking.

For I have no home to call mine, no shelter to lie under
Exposed to nature's harsh winds and embraced by its thunder
A nomad with no purpose, I have been made to wander
Chased by my sins, that from my lover tore me sunder
And left our love bare for enemies to plunder
Where is our supposed 'forever' now, my love? I really do wonder.

Osalam Wosu

ABOUT THE POETS

Vincethapoet (Vincent Joseph Osbourne)

I remember I was 14 and I lived in Compton, California. I was walking down the street to 7-Eleven and out of nowhere a police car almost ran me over. The cop hopped out the car and slammed me on the hood of his car and jammed his gun in my side. I remember the hood of the car burning my skin but I wasn't afraid. I remember that day like yesterday; He pulled my wallet out of my back pocket and looked at my ID. He then threw the ID back at me. I pick up my wallet and yelled, "What the FUCK did I do?" He just got back in the car and drove off. I knew it was something wrong about society when that happened. Today I live in Portland, Oregon. I spent time working as an electrical helper and working at various production jobs as a supervisor. Fortunately, I haven't experienced such direct injustice as when I lived in California; I have experienced quite a bit of indirect racism here. What I learned in this quasi- progressive climate is being black can hold you back or move you forward- it really depends on your perception. I want everyone who reads this book to consider the different perspectives of black people that live in today's world. Many times, our surroundings may seem like the entire world, but the diversity amongst black people in this book will hopefully help you see that you can create your very own world of opportunity. Please enjoy this book and, if you're moved by it, please share this book with someone you love. – Vincethapoet on all platforms.

Osalam C. Wosu

Osalam Wosu is a graduate of chemical engineering from the Federal University of Technology Owerri, Nigeria. He binges on deep poetry that is inspired by topics that hurt to speak of – heartbreak, mourning, hatred and fear. He was shortlisted for the Korean Nigerian Poetry Fiesta Award in 2017 and also in 2019, and has his works in various online platforms and in the Mounting the Moon Anthology of Queer Nigerian Poems (edited by Unoma Azuah). He writes and blogs from Port Harcourt, Nigeria.

"This anthology in all its entirety is meant to serve as a beacon and awake up call to the tempests of the average black person in this present age. The voice of this collection and the poems I contributed are to serve as a moral confluence of the lives of black people in a world where we are seldom motivated. I hope to teach that by embracing our uniqueness we can unite in the similarities of our trials and speak with one voice, embrace expressionism and together forge a better culture for an even better future."

Adegunloye Kayode

"My name is Adegunloye Kayode, a graduate of English and literary studies and equally a Masters in view student in International relations. I'm currently the lead senior contributing officer at Gleetz magazine, the community engagement coordinator at Ambassadors of Africa (AOA) which is a group of young Africans who are zealous about ensuring a better life for less privileged persons across Africa. I also own a mini blog which I named Edoyaksdiary, which encompass various gists about life, society, poems, relationships and some of my personal activities. I'm also looking to author my first book this year. I'm just a lover of anything arts.

Furthermore, my advice to youths and young ones alike about being black is that they should enjoy their colour, it's nothing short of beautiful to carry and wear that colour graciously. It will be foolhardy to give ears to bleaching and trying to ditch their melanin, especially in this 21st century and this year 2019. Hence I encourage them to see themselves as different from the rest, and of course with a touch of class. Black is the real deal!"

Priye (K.O)

So, we are here to learn about PRIYE who is popularly known as K.O or kofowrites. Prepare to be bored, well not because she is totally amazing and funny and cool and oh golly. I cannot control myself when talking about her highness.

Priye is the second child of her single mother. Priye, her 2 sisters and mom were abandoned by their father because their mother bore only girls.

She has a blog: (koforolablog.wordpress.com) and you can find her on IG @kofowrites or twitter @K.O. PRIYE is a lover of mathematics and construction of buildings and physics. She has a book on Wattpad (HWC) she is currently trying to pursue a career in engineering or architecture.

Priye started writing at the early age of 8 (her mom says she has been writing since she was 3). Well funny thing is her father was the one who brought out the writer in her. She hates him to the core and is presently trying to get over it but she will forever acknowledge this thing he did for her.

Ending this short biography- remember what PRIYE wrote on her IG anytime you feel neglected or treated badly.

"YOU SHOULD HAVE MADE HASTE WHILE THE SUN SHONE. NOW THE WHOLE HOST OF HEAVEN IS HERE AND THEY DANCE TO MY FAVOUR."

Salim Sulaiman Liman

Salim Sulaiman Liman is a 21-year-old student of computer sciences in Ahmadu Bello University, Zaria, Nigeria. A human of many passions, amongst them is writing. "What does he do as a profession?" He spends much of his time building himself being optimistic that he will be a professional writer and a sound scientist in his future days.

He was born in Africa, in Nigeria to be precise. His part of the earth is a nation with cultural and religious diversity. He demands himself to live a life with zero discrimination fueled by differences, as he once said in his poem, "There is a lamp inside me and I shall not give its light to a single tribe or religion but to earth and all her citizens," (from the poem "A Poet's Spirit" via Instagram). Humanity is his ruling fire above all and he pleads with younger ones to house inside them the same love for humanity above all differences.

"Concerning my poem contributions to this book, my raw ideologies and the world from my eyes are my muses as well as the world from the eyes of others. This is my first book project. I, with hope in heart, hope you find my contributions meaningful and the book too, entirely. Thank you!"

Made in the USA
Monee, IL
03 June 2020